EASTER

Meditations on the Resurrection

Raniero Cantalamessa, O.F.M. Cap.

EASTER
Meditations on the Resurrection

Translated by Demetrio S. Yocum

LITURGICAL PRESS
Collegeville, Minnesota

www.litpress.org

This book was originally published by Edizione San Paolo, Milan, Italy, under the title *Pasqua: Un passaggio a cio che non passa.*

Cover design by Ann Blattner. *The Resurrection,* Dieric Bouts, 1455.

1   2   3   4   5   6   7

Library of Congress Cataloging-in-Publication Data

Cantalamessa, Raniero.
    Easter : meditations on the Resurrection / Raniero Cantalamessa ; translated by Demetrio S. Yocum.
        p.   cm.
    ISBN-13: 978-0-8146-2706-8 (alk. paper)
    ISBN-10: 0-8146-2706-4 (alk. paper)
    1. Easter—Meditations.   Paschal mystery—Meditations.   3. Jesus Christ—Resurrection—Meditations.   I. Title.

BV55.C3213   2006
242'.36—dc22

                                                                2006000602

Contents

Introduction

This book is composed of four meditations on the paschal mystery (given to the Pontifical Household in the presence of Pope John Paul II, the cardinals, the bishops, and the prelates of the Roman Curia during Lent of 2004) together with the homily given in St. Peter's Basilica on Good Friday of the same year, during the Liturgy of the Lord's Passion at which John Paul II presided.

The author has dealt several times with the subject from an historical perspective, at the time when he was Professor of Ancient Christianity at the Catholic University of Milan,[1] as well as from a pastoral and spiritual one, as the official Preacher to the Pontifical Household.[2]

Numquam satis! There can never be enough talk about the paschal mystery, as it is the heart, so to speak, of Christian faith. In the following meditations I return to the subject from a pastoral and spiritual viewpoint, but this time following a new and different path, indicated by the traditional doctrine of the four senses of the Scriptures: historical, christological, moral, and eschatological. Such an attempt may be seen as a way to reach the center of a circle by moving in succession from four different points on its circumference, or to get to a city's center by entering from four different gates. What an ancient author said of God is appropriate for the paschal mystery as well, "Such a great mystery cannot be reached by following only one path."

In Good Friday's homily, which brings to an end the cycle of meditations, the paschal mystery is briefly investigated starting from the Servant Song in Deutero-Isaiah, with particular attention to the question, so profoundly felt today, of the relation between violence and the sacred.

Not only is the paschal mystery an idea, a doctrine, or an institution; it is, in its essence, a person, the dead and risen Jesus Christ. Hence, St. Gregory Nazianzen's famous exultation, which inspired me in writing the following meditations, becomes clear:

---

[1] R. Cantalamessa, *Easter in the Early Church* (Collegeville: Liturgical Press, 1993).

[2] R. Cantalamessa, *The Mystery of Easter* (Collegeville: Liturgical Press, 1993).

"O Pascha, great and sacred, the purification of the whole world—
I will speak of you as of a living person."[3]

[3] St. Gregory Nazianzen, *Oratio* 45, 30 (PG 36, 664 A).

"THE LETTER TEACHES THE FACTS"

The Historical Dimension of Easter

There has been, in the Christian tradition as a whole, a twofold approach to the reading of the Scriptures, which can be epitomized in the words "letter" and "Spirit." "Letter" refers to the literal sense or to the narrated historical event, while "Spirit" points to the mystery hidden in the historical event. The spiritual sense, in turn, comprises three different levels of meaning: the christological, which brings to light the reference to Christ and the church; the moral, which refers to Christian conduct; and the eschatological which is concerned with the ultimate events.

The final four-part scheme was summarized in a famous distich, *"Littera gesta docet, quid credas allegoria. / Moralis quid agas; quo tendas anagogia."* (The *letter* teaches the facts; *allegory* what to believe; the *moral* sense teaches how to act; and the *anagogical* what to aim at.) I would like to explore the meaning of Christ's Pasch by following this method handed down to us by the most constant tradition of the church.

In the first meditation, which follows, we take into consideration the historical dimension of Easter, i.e., the events from which it stemmed. If we were to reflect on Easter in general, the "letter" we would have to examine would be the accounts of Exodus which narrate the sacrifice of the lamb in Egypt. But since our focus is the Christian Easter, the "letter" is represented by the Gospel narratives of the passion and resurrection of Christ.

1. But does the letter really teach the facts?

At this point, a topical question arises: in this case, does the letter really teach, as the ancient distich says, "the facts," or does it offer instead a "tendentious" version, responding to apologetic intents? In this regard, on the occasion of the release of Mel Gibson's film *The Passion of Christ,* a theory has been advanced which cannot be left unanswered. In brief, according to this theory—widely spread by the international press—a representation of the Passion rigorously based on the Gospel narratives ignores the results of modern exegetical science. The latter claims that in referring to the events, Mark, with the other evangelists following him, held the Jews responsible for Christ's death to win Rome's favor and, at the same time, to reassure Roman authorities about the new religion. In reality, the main reason for Jesus' sentence had to do with political and not religious causes, since he was considered a threat to public order.[1] ·

First of all, it must be said that whatever interpretation is given to the external circumstances and the juridical motives behind Christ's death, they do not in the least undermine its true meaning which was determined by what he, and not others, thought. Jesus made clear in advance the meaning he had given to his death when he instituted the Eucharist: "Take it and eat, this is my body given for you."

That having been said, the seriousness of what is at stake in such discussions should not be undermined. Christian faith is a faith based on history; its compatibility with history is no less necessary than its logical coherence. It is not enough to say that the Gospels "didn't fall fully formed from the sky but are the product of human hands and hearts," equally exposed to partialities and prejudices. Any serious biblical scholar today would admit this. The question is to determine if they are to be trusted or not; whether the prejudice is an unconscious one, or the theory is deliberately favored and perpetrated to achieve a certain advantage.

Having dealt with the problem at the time I was teaching the history of ancient Christianity at the Catholic University of Milan,[2] I feel obliged, in my small way, to shed some light on the subject. What must be vigorously contested, with regard to Christ's death sentence,

---

[1] See John Meacham, "Who killed Jesus?" *Newsweek* (February 16, 2004) 49–57.

[2] See the results of the research on "I primi cristiani, la politica e lo stato" in fasc. *Vita e Pensiero* 6, year 54 (November–December 1972), in particular "Gesu' e la Rivoluzione," 5–18, and "Dieci anni di studi sul processo di Gesu' e su Gesu' e gli zeloti," 108–136.

is the fact that modern historical research has reached conclusions different from those drawn from the reading of the Gospels.

Over the last fifty years the essentially political theory of Christ's sentence has stemmed from two preoccupations and has had two *Sitz-im-Leben.* The first is represented by the *Shoah,* the tragic epilogue of anti-Semitism; the second, by the emergence of the so-called revolution theology in the sixties and seventies, which naively attempted to make Che Guevara one of Jesus' disciples, lest he replace Jesus in the hearts of younger generations.

Basically, both positions, though in distinct ways, reached a similar conclusion: Jesus was a supporter of the Zealot movement planning to overthrow by force Roman domination, together with its local sympathizers present among the wealthy classes. Proof of this was derived from the fact that one of his disciples' names was Simon "the Zealot" (similarly, by calling another disciple Matthew "the Publican," it may be argued that Jesus was a collaborator of the Romans!); that another, Judas, was nicknamed "Iscariot," which could be a deformation of "Sicariot"—the name which designated the radical wing of the Zealot party; and other episodes like the expulsion of the dealers from the temple; the messianic entrance in Jerusalem; the miracle of the loaves; the attempt to make him king, etc.

In a very few years the "revolutionary Jesus" theory was rejected as untenable. It ended up attributing to Jesus the idea of a Messiah who imposes himself by force, an idea which he in fact refused throughout his whole life. The other position, however, the one aspiring to remove any hint of anti-Semitism, was maintained.

Although this may be considered a worthy concern, it is also well known that the greatest damage that can be done to a just cause is that of defending it with the wrong arguments. The struggle against anti-Semitism is founded on a more solid basis than such a questionable supposition. The Second Vatican Council put it as follows: "True, the Jewish authorities and those who followed their lead pressed for the death of Christ; still, what happened in His passion cannot be charged against all the Jews then alive, without distinction, nor against the Jews of today."[3]

---

[3] Declaration on the Relation of the Church to Non-Christian Religions, *Nostra aetate,* 4.

This position is quite in line with the past Jewish tradition itself. What emerges from the accounts of the *Talmud* as well as other Jewish sources (however late and historically disputable) on Jesus' death is the fact that the Jewish tradition never denied the responsibility of the public authorities of the time in sentencing Jesus to death. It did not base its defense on the denial of the fact, but rather on the point that, from a Jewish perspective, the sentence was not an unjust one and it constituted no offense.[4]

This version is compatible with that of the New Testament sources which, on one hand, hold Jewish public authorities responsible for Christ's sentence, and on the other absolve them by blaming their ignorance (see Luke 23:34; Acts 3:17; 1 Cor 2:8). Only God, who reads our hearts, knows to what extent such ignorance was due to objective difficulty in recognizing as true Christ's messianic claim or due to other, less justifiable reasons (John 5:44 among other reasons, mentions vanity). It is not given to any of us to bring in a verdict against Judas, or Caiaphas, or Pilate.

An essential observation is this: no formula of faith of either the New Testament or the church states that Jesus died "for the sins *of the Jews.*" The fundamental truth is that he "died for *our* sins," i.e., the sins of all.

The evidence that the Jewish people, as such, had nothing to do with Christ's death stands on a biblical grounding shared with Christians, yet surprisingly forgotten for many centuries: "Only the one who sins shall die. The son shall not be charged with the guilt of his father, nor shall the father be charged with the guilt of his son" (Ezek 18:20). The doctrine of the church acknowledges only one sin bequeathed from father to son: original sin.

If the future generations of Jews were held responsible for Christ's death, the same should have been said, adding the charge of deicide, of the future generations of Romans, since it is certain that, from a juridical stance, Christ's sentence and his execution (the procedure of crucifixion confirms it) are to be imputed, in the last analysis, to the Roman authorities.

Perhaps we believers are asked to go a step beyond merely asserting the innocence of the Jewish people, and to recognize in their unjust suffering throughout history their share in the fate of

---

[4] See J. Blinzler, *The Trial of Jesus* (Cork: Mercier, 1959).

God's suffering Servant, who, for Christians, is Jesus. This is how Edith Stein foresaw the tragedy awaiting her and her people in Hitler's Germany: "There, under the cross, I understood the destiny of God's people. I said to myself: those who realize that this is Christ's cross ought to bear it themselves, on behalf of all others."

2. Can we still believe in the passion narratives?

Having refuted the charge of anti-Semitism, we can turn our attention to the reliability of the passion narratives, which is of interest to us here. I would like to recall some facts which invite us to consider with prudence the thesis which says that the passion narratives were written to reassure the Roman imperial authorities about Christians.

This thesis ends up placing the apostolic documents within the apologetic genre inaugurated by second-century Christian authors writing to Roman emperors to convince them of the goodness of the new religion. What is neglected is the fact that the apostolic documents were written for the Christian community, without having in mind readers outside of it—who in fact never existed. (The first pagan author who shows he had read Christian sources is Celsus, in the second century, and certainly not for political reasons.)

We know that the passion narratives circulated, in shorter units and in oral form, within the communities well before the final editing of the Gospels, Mark included. Paul the Apostle, in his earliest letter, written about the year 50 C.E., gives the same basic account of Christ's death present in the Gospels (see 1 Thess 2:15). Having from the very beginning approved and strenuously endorsed the Nazarene's sentence, he was much better acquainted than us moderns with the events which occurred shortly before his arrival in Jerusalem.

At this earlier stage, Christianity still considered itself destined primarily for Israel; the communities in which the first traditions took form consisted basically of converted Jews; Matthew's main concern is to show that Jesus has come to fulfill, and not abolish, the Law. Therefore, should an apologetic preoccupation be found, the attempt would have been to present pagans, and not the Jewish authorities, as responsible for Christ's sentence, thus reassuring the Jews of Palestine and of the Diaspora about Christians.

Much confusion arises from the fact that we project the future opposition between Jews and Christians onto the early period of the church, whereas, before the increase of mainly Gentile communities, the real opposition was between Jews who believed in Christ and those who did not. The distinction cuts across the communal Jewish identity. Jesus' disciples could have said with Paul the Apostle, "Are they Hebrews? So am I" (2 Cor 11:22). This gives the anti-Jewish polemic of the authors of the New Testament a very different meaning from that of later Christianity, the same way the invectives of Moses and the prophets against the people of Israel are different from those of certain church fathers or of Luther.

On the other hand, when Mark and the other evangelists wrote their Gospels, Nero's persecution had already taken place, and this may have led them to see Jesus as the first victim of Roman domination and Christian martyrs as those sharing their Lord's same fate. The book of Revelation, written after Domitian's persecution, attests to such a vision by offering a fierce invective against Rome ("Babylon," the "Beast," the "prostitute") stained with the martyrs' blood (see Rev 13ff.).

The passion narratives cannot be read without considering what preceded them. Every single page of the Gospel attests to the growing religious clash between Jesus and an influential group of Jews (Pharisees, priests, scribes) on several issues: the observance of the Sabbath; attitudes toward sinners and publicans; clean and unclean. Joachim Jeremias has pointed out the anti-Pharisaic motivation present in almost all the parables of Jesus.[5] This background cannot be eliminated without completely demolishing the Gospels and making them incomprehensible. But having acknowledged this conflict, how can one think that it did not play an important role in the final settling of the score, and that the Jewish authorities decided to denounce Jesus to Pilate almost reluctantly, only for fear of a Roman armed intervention?

One of the most accredited arguments against the veracity of the Gospel narratives is the way Pilate is represented in them. Far from being a man sensitive to reasons of justice, who is concerned about the fate of an unknown Jew, it has been proved instead that

---

[5] See Joachim Jeremias, *The Parables of Jesus* (London: SMC Press, 1963) or (New York: Scribner's, 1972).

he was hard and cruel, ready to crush in a bloodbath the slightest sign of revolt.

However, there is a mistake here. Pilate does not attempt to save Jesus out of compassion, but rather out of spite against the victim's accusers with whom he was at loggerheads since his arrival in Judea. If the first Christians were mistaken in something, it was in attributing to Pilate's behavior sentiments of justice and compassion toward Jesus. (According to Tertullian, he was secretly a Christian, while the Coptic Church canonized him together with his wife!) In reality, his only concern was not to give in to the hated Jewish leadership. If one reads the dialogue between him and Jesus' accusers with a minimum of psychological introspection, it becomes clear that the evangelists did not overlook his true motivation.

In conclusion it should be remembered how in the postwar years the debate over the reasons for Christ's sentence produced countless, often contrasting, critical hypotheses, but without convincing the majority of historians on any important point. Every time a solution to a problem was proposed, a thousand other problems appeared. Some, for example, questioned the historical veracity of Jesus being called before the Sanhedrin. But if this is the case, then the most certainly true episode of Peter's denial, which is inextricably linked in time and setting to that circumstance, cannot be proved either.

Undoubtedly, the Gospel narratives present many incongruous details and obscure passages, but it is precisely these that attest to the "genuineness" of accounts which stem from the life and memories of different persons rather than from attempts to support a thesis. A mark of honesty is provided by the poor figure the authors and witnesses themselves cut in them: one, the leader, repudiates; another betrays; while the rest, at the moment of the arrest, flee ignominiously. The biblical scholar Lucien Cerfaux was not far from the truth when he used to say, "The simplest way to read the Gospel is often also the most accurate."[6]

This leaves open the question about the use that is made of the evangelical material. The inaccuracy, as well as the anti-Jewish distortions, with which it has been used in the past has been largely acknowledged today and firmly rebuked by the church in

---

[6] Lucien Cerfaux, *Jesus aux origines de la tradition* (Louvain, 1968).

appropriate documents. In the light of the observations made so far, we may conclude by saying that a representation of the Passion is misleading if it implies that all the Jews at that time, and those who came after, are to be held responsible for Christ's death. Yet, historical truth is by no means compromised if one admits that an influential group of Jews took a crucial part in it.

3. Jesus was silent

If divergence of positions is still present with regard to the role and behavior of various characters and powerful groups involved in Christ's Passion at least there is unanimity about him and his conduct. Sovereign dignity, calm, and absolute freedom: not one gesture or word to contradict what he had preached in his Gospel, especially in the Beatitudes.

And yet, there was nothing in him to remind us of the Stoic's proud contempt of pain. More than human is his reaction to suffering and cruelty: in Gethsemane, he trembles while his sweat falls like blood; he prays to be delivered from the cup awaiting him; he seeks comfort from his disciples; he cries out his distress on the cross, "My God, my God, why have you forsaken me?" (Mark 15:34).

A film of a few years ago, *The Last Temptation of Christ,* depicts Jesus on the Cross wrestling with carnal temptations. The psychological absurdity of such a representation was justly remarked. If Jesus could be tempted while hanging on the Cross—racked by pain and insulted by his enemies—it certainly would have nothing to do with being tempted in the flesh. He would, rather, have been tempted by hatred for the violence inflicted on him, or by feelings of anger and dreams of vengeance.

The Psalter was there to provide him with scathing words, "Arise, Lord, destroy them, defeat them." But he quoted none of the psalms of imprecation, nor did he appeal to his Father for "twelve legions of angels," though he knew they would have been immediately granted him (see Matt 26:53). As we read in Peter's first letter, "When he was insulted, he returned no insult; when he suffered, he did not threaten; instead, he handed himself over to the one who judges justly" (1 Pet 2:23).

You can spend a lifetime immersed in the perfection of Christ's holiness and still not come to the end. In Christ we face the infinite in the ethical order. There is no memory of a similar death in the history of the world. In meditating on the Passion, one should be touched by Jesus' holiness more than by the evil and iniquity of those surrounding him. In his Apostolic Letter on the beginning of the New Millennium *(Novo Millennio Ineunte)* the Pope invites us to contemplate "the sorrowful face of the Redeemer." That face itself is a book, the whole Bible on a single page.

I would like to highlight a trait of Christ's supernatural glory during his Passion: his silence. *"Jesus autem tacebat,"* i.e., "But Jesus was silent" (Matt 26:63). He is silent in front of Caiaphas; his silence irritates Pilate; he keeps silent in front of Herod who wished instead to see some miracle worked by him (see Luke 23:8).

Jesus' silence is neither deliberate nor accusing. He does not leave unanswered specific questions in which truth is at stake, yet even on such occasions his are just a few essential words, uttered without anger. Silence in him is totally and only love.

Jesus' silence during the Passion is the key to understanding the silence of God. When "Babel's noise" becomes too great, the only way of saying something is to be silent. Jesus' silence in fact disturbs, irritates, and reveals the untruth of words themselves, as when he kept silent facing the accusers of the adulteress.

"What cannot be expressed, should be left silent." If, on the one hand, this famous slogan of linguistic positivism helped to exclude (in spite of the author's own intention) the possibility of any statement concerning God as well as theology itself, on the other hand, it becomes extremely true and profound if applied to Jesus. "Many are the things I would like to tell you; better still, just one, but greater than the sea," exclaims the heroine of a lyrical opera of Puccini who is about to die. These words could be put into Jesus' mouth. Only one thing had he to say, but so great that people were not ready to receive it. He had tried to say the word to Pilate—the word "Truth!"—but we all know with what result.

This first meditation on the historical dimension of Easter, i.e., the "letter," is not the right place for the moral applications that will follow. As individuals, we should all reflect instead on the meaning this trait of silence, revealed by Christ during his Passion, takes on in our own life as well as in that of the church. However, what is in line with the historical observations we have elaborated is for us to open our soul to a boundless veneration, enthusiasm, and gratitude to Christ. Touched by his infinite love and the majesty of his suffering, we cry from the bottom of our hearts, *"Adoramus te, Christe, et benedicimus tibi, quia per sanctam crucem tuam redemisti mundum.* We adore you, O Christ, and bless you, because with your holy Cross, you have saved the world."

2

ALLEGORY TEACHES WHAT TO BELIEVE

The Easter of Faith

1. The spiritual reading of the Bible

After the historical approach to the paschal mystery of the first meditation, we now move on to deal with the spiritual sense enclosed in the "letter" of the paschal narratives. Let us follow St. Augustine who said, *"Factum audivimus, mysterium requiramus."*[1] We came to know what happened; let us now inquire after the mystery.

The spiritual reading of the Scriptures began with Jesus. What else was he doing with the two disciples on the road to Emmaus other than explaining "what referred to him in all the scriptures?" (Luke 24:27). Such practice continued with the apostles and has permeated the subsequent life of the church in its various expressions: exegesis, theology, liturgy, art, and spirituality. It still nourishes Christian life today, through its derivative method of *lectio divina* as well as through the liturgy and the lives of the saints.

John Paul II's apostolic letter proclaiming St. Therese of the Infant Jesus Doctor of the Church, states:

> Despite her inadequate training and lack of resources for studying and interpreting the sacred books, Thérèse immersed herself in meditation on the Word of God with exceptional faith and spontaneity. Under the influence of the Holy Spirit she attained a profound knowledge of Revelation for herself and for others. By her loving concentration on Scripture — she even wanted to learn Hebrew and Greek to understand better the spirit and letter of the sacred books — she showed the importance of the

---

[1] St. Augustine, *In Ioh.* 50, 6 (PL 35, 1760).

biblical sources in the spiritual life, she emphasized the origi-
nality and freshness of the Gospel, she cultivated with modera-
tion the spiritual exegesis of the Word of God in both the Old
and New Testaments.[2]

St. Therese never had at her disposal either an integral text of
the Bible nor any of the modern resources to study it. As regards
"scientific" knowledge, she knew less than the most recent student
enrolled at the Biblical Institute in Rome; yet who would dare say
there is anyone who knew the Bible better than she?

The example of the Saint of Lisieux well exemplifies the attitude with which this spiritual way of reading the Bible contrasts
with the scientific approaches. There is no disdain or disregard for
the latter, of course. On the contrary, the scientific methods should
inspire unlimited respect together with a desire to derive the greatest profit from them as well as gratitude for whoever puts them at
our disposal—though always as instruments and means to reach
a different type of understanding. They should not be regarded as
the final word on the Bible, but as the first. Henri de Lubac, who
wrote the classical works on this patristic and medieval exegesis
of the Bible, clearly emphasizes this point.[3]

As regards the spiritual sense, one can give emphasis to the theological, the moral, or the eschatological dimension. Let us recall
the famous distich, *"Littera gesta docet, quid credas allegoria. /
Moralis quid agas; quo tendas anagogia."* (The *letter* teaches the
facts; *allegory* teaches what to believe; the *moral* sense teaches
how to act; and the *anagogical* what to aim at.) Today we will
consider the allegorical sense of Easter, namely, what to believe.

The term "allegory" is not very popular among scholars nowa-
days; or rather, it arouses innumerable doubts due to the use, and
abuse, made of it in the past. But in the best exegesis of the fathers, the concept of allegory has a completely different meaning
from the one present in pagan authors and from its modern usage.
It does not refer to a physical object or historical fact symbolizing

---

[2] Apostolic letter *Divini amoris scientia,* 19 October 1997.

[3] See Henri de Lubac, *Exégèse médiévale. Les quatre sens de l'Ecriture,* I,1
(Paris: Aubier, 1959) 127ff.; Engl. transl. *Medieval Exegesis: The Four Senses of
Scripture,* I/1, trans. Mark Sebanc (Grand Rapids: William B. Eerdmans Publish-
ing Company, 1998).

a spiritual and eternal idea, but rather a true fact, or partial truth, tending toward a future fulfillment. The correlation is not vertical, as the correlation between the physical object and its eternal idea in Plato's system, but horizontal and located in time, as it is between two events where one announces and prepares the other. History is not nullified here to the advantage of the spirit, but the latter uses it as support. In this sense, Paul the Apostle, talking about the first covenant represented by Hagar, says that it was an "allegory" of the new covenant represented by Sara (see Gal 4:24). The abuse of the allegorical method began when this very specific biblical meaning was forgotten in order to launch into all sorts of abstruse speculations on numbers and words.

When dealing with texts and events of the Old Testament Christian allegory consists in drawing attention to their references to Christ; when words or truths in the New Testament are taken into account, Christian allegory consists in drawing attention to their mystical meaning for the church, as it is particularly clear in the wording of the *kerygma*. In the statement "He died for our sins and was raised for our justification" "He died" and "He was raised" are facts—historical in their own way; "for our sins" and "for our justification" are not historical assertions, but assertions of faith; they point at the mystical sense of the facts "for us."

When you really think of it, it is precisely this meaning of faith which somehow transforms the death and resurrection of Christ into "historical" events, if by "historical" fact we refer not merely to the plain event but to the *fact* and its *meaning*. There are countless facts which really took place, and yet are not "historical" because they left no trace in history and did not arouse any interest or give birth to anything new. "An event is historical when it combines two elements: it "happened" and, *what's more*, it took on such a relevant significance for the people involved that it had to be told."[4]

In this sense, Christ's death is the most "historical" event in world history because it influenced humanity more than any other event. We have recently seen with the release of Mel Gibson's film on the Passion of Christ how this event, with all that it entails, can still stir up consciences and arouse divergent opinions.

---

[4] D.H. Dodd, *History and the Gospel* (London: James Nisbet & Co., 1964²).

2. *A new age begins*

The first to explore in an unsurpassed way the theological meaning of Christ's paschal event was Paul the Apostle. From this point of view, the letter to the Romans represents the culminating point of his speculation. After presenting, in the first two chapters of the letter, humanity in its universal condition of sin and perdition ("Jews and Greeks alike . . . are all under the domination of sin . . . all have sinned and are deprived of the glory of God" [Rom 3:9, 23]), he shows an incredible audacity by proclaiming that this situation is now radically changed, forever and for all: "They are justified freely by his grace through the redemption in Christ Jesus" (Rom 3:24). A new age in the history of the relationship between God and humanity begins—a momentous change indeed.

Paul the Apostle draws attention to two distinctive elements in the salvation performed by Christ, though they are inseparable as two sides of the same coin: a negative component, which consists in the forgiveness of sin or justification of sinners (Rom 3–7), and a positive one, consisting in the gift of the Spirit and the new life it entails (Rom 8).

This distinction is invariably at work in both the Old and New Testaments every time a succinct description of salvation is provided. In Ezekiel 36:25-26 the negative element "I will sprinkle clean water upon you to cleanse you from all your impurities, and from all your idols I will cleanse you . . . taking from your bodies your stony hearts" is completed by the positive element "I will give you a new heart, and place a new spirit within you." The verbs employed are *to take* and *to give*. Presenting Jesus to the world John the Baptist says, "Behold, the Lamb of God, who takes away the sin of the world" (the negative element), but he soon adds, "he is the one who will baptize with the holy Spirit" (John 1: 29, 33). Peter does the same on the day of Pentecost, proclaiming, "Repent and be baptized, every one of you, in the name of Jesus Christ for the forgiveness of your sins; and you will receive the gift of the holy Spirit" (Acts 2:38).

In the past, the theological disputes that arose from commenting on the letter to the Romans drew an almost exclusive attention to the negative element, i.e., the forgiveness of sin, to the detriment of the positive one. But in reality, between the two aspects of salvation—the justification of sinners and the gift of the Holy Spirit—it is the second moment of salvation that occupies a more relevant position for Paul. In all his letters he refers to it, whereas he mentions the justification by faith only in the letters written to defend his mission among the Gentiles. Worth noticing is the fact that it is one of the most competent Protestant exegetes of our time to state this.[5]

When, after discussing the deliverance from sin and the law, at the beginning of chapter 8 of the letter to the Romans, Paul starts to write about the gift of the Spirit, he gives the impression of having finally reached his goal and can abandon himself to a free song. It is a moment which recalls Beethoven's choral hymn of joy introducing the second part of the Ninth Symphony, "O friends, not these sounds! But let us strike up pleasanter, and more joyful music."[6] Consider the following words of Paul:

> For the law of the spirit of life in Christ Jesus has freed you from the law of sin and death . . . but you are not in the flesh; on the contrary, you are in the spirit. . . . The Spirit itself bears witness with our spirit that we are children of God . . . the Spirit too comes to the aid of our weakness (Rom 8:2, 9, 16, 26).

The justification of sinners and the forgiveness of sin are for Paul nothing else but the condition for receiving the most beautiful and perfect gift of Christ's Easter, i.e., his Spirit. Many are persuaded that the rise and overwhelming expansion of the Pentecostal and Charismatic movements within the various Christian churches should also be regarded as a reaction against a too unilateral insistence on justification by faith to the detriment of the doctrine and experience of the Spirit. This "third force," as it is called, in little more than a century has surprisingly increased and today it represents, according to statistics, "the fastest growing component within Christianity."

This "third force" may ultimately help to find the solution to problems long unsolved, problems for which not even the document co-signed by the Catholic and the Lutheran World Federation has been able to offer a full agreement. According to the theology and spirituality of the Pentecostal movement, justification by faith

---

[5] See J.D.G. Dunn, *The Theology of Paul, the Apostle* (Cambridge: Eerdmans, 1998).

[6] *"O Freunde, nicht diese Tñe! Sondern laßt uns angenehmere anstimmen und freudenvollere!"*

is not merely an exterior charge of justice leaving the believer unchanged *(simul iustus et peccator);* the claim, as it is for Catholics (even though it is not always explicitly stated), is that the believer is really transformed by the Holy Spirit's gift of a new heart and by the Spirit's dwelling within it.

When Paul writes about the Holy Spirit—even the most rigorous exegetes agree on this point—he defines it as a common experience shared by everyone within the church, and not only as a doctrine. As such, it is an experience of grace that flows from the proclamation of the message; of awareness of being God's children in prayer; of charismatic power in one's own ministry; of comfort in tribulation. It is on this experiential basis that one assesses whether the Holy Spirit has regained its true place in the life of the church, not only by way of theology.

Sad indeed would it be if the experience of the Spirit were confined within one single ecclesiastical movement without being shared, in substance if not in form, by all the church as a salutary "current of grace" going through her body. All those baptized in the church are in need of a new Pentecost, not only a few.

3. An awakening of faith

As the ancient distich says, allegory teaches "what to believe," *quid credas.* But it is not enough to have determined the object of paschal faith, "the things which are believed, the content" or *fides quae,* namely, the forgiveness of sin and the gift of the Spirit; the intensity with which one believes, defined in theology as "the act by which one believes" or *fides qua,* ought to be our concern as well.

Even in this respect Paul the Apostle is our model. His words reveal how the paschal mystery can become the true meaning of Christian life, "yet I live, no longer I, but Christ lives in me; insofar as I now live in the flesh, I live by faith in the Son of God who has loved me and given himself up for me" (Gal 2:20).

At present, we hear a lot about "existential faith." What can we do to awaken, increase it, if it is basically God's gift and beyond our own will? We must start to rekindle our wonder in front of it. In an African-American spiritual there is this line, "But I am praying, I can pray!" as though one, in amazement, realizes one is doing something considered impossible, like "I am flying." We must do the same with faith: become aware of the infinite, extraordinary privilege that such a gift represents and, in wonder, endlessly thank God the Father for it, thus crying out for joy, like the man born blind and cured by Jesus, "he opened my eyes" (John 9:30).

What comes to pass every morning in the visible world at sunrise should transpire within us every day at the rising of the Sun-Christ. "Kindle in us faith, hope, and love," a hymn at morning Lauds makes us say. A terrible mistake would be to take for granted the gift of faith, as though, having believed once, we are forever safe. On the contrary, such gift must be kept "with fear and trembling." The parable of the ten virgins reminds us that we can keep holding the lamp all our life without realizing that its light is extinguished.

As I was once reflecting on faith, I said to myself, "It's a shame that there is no hymn to faith comparable with Paul's hymn to charity!" but suddenly I realized that such a hymn already exists and is written by someone even greater than Paul:

> "If you have faith the size of a mustard seed" (Matt 17:20).

> "If you can! Everything is possible to one who has faith!" (Mark 9:23).

> "Let it be done for you according to your faith" (Matt 9:29).

> "Did I not tell you that if you believe you will see the glory of God?" (John 11:40).

> "Whoever believes in me, even if he dies, will live" (John 11:25).

> "Repent, and believe in the gospel" (Mark 1:15).

> "Whoever believes and is baptized will be saved" (Mark 16:16).

The entire Gospel is a hymn to faith. I would like to share with you an "explosive" moment of such faith which I happened to experience—because there is nothing of it which I can boast about, as though it came from me. On Christmas 2002 I was at the Midnight Mass presided by John Paul II in St. Peter's Basilica. It was the moment of the singing of the Roman Martyrology's announcement of Christ's birth:

> Many centuries after the creation of the world . . .
>
> Thirteen centuries after the flight from Egypt . . .
>
> In the year 752 after Rome's foundation . . .
>
> In the forty-second year of Caesar Augustus' empire, Jesus Christ, eternal God and Son of the eternal Father, conceived by the power of the Holy Spirit, after nine months, was born in Bethlehem in Judea of the Virgin Mary, and became man.

At these last words, I experienced what is usually referred to as a "breakthrough in faith," i.e., a sudden inner illumination after which you say to yourself, "It's true! It's all true! They're not just words. On the contrary, words reveal but a very small part of the reality. God dwelt among us indeed." I was completely pervaded by a sudden joy, unable to say anything else than just, "Thank you, Father! Thank you, Jesus! Thank you, too, Mother of God!"

I believe that all of us can experience a similar moment during the Easter vigil, while listening to the words of the *Exsultet*, "This is the night when Jesus Christ broke the chains of death and rose triumphant from the grave." The first step is to listen carefully, as though we hear those words for the first time. Let us not forget that, *Fides ex auditu*, "faith comes from what is heard" (Rom 10:17).

The saying of the Scriptures, "the just man, because of his faith, shall live" (cf. Hab 2:4; Rom 1:17) is particularly indicated for church ministers as well as for messengers of the Gospel. God's servants' true worth lies in their faith. What believers immediately grasp of him, or her, is if "they believe": if they believe in what they say and celebrate. Faith is contagious: as no infection occurs by simply talking about or studying a virus, but only after contact, so it is with faith.

A theme most precious among the fathers of the church was Easter as the rebirth of nature. They saw an analogy between nature in springtime and our souls at Easter. St. Zeno of Verona exclaims, "This day, once last winter's gloom has gone, under the mild breathing of the gentle wind Favonius, everywhere the fields are in bloom, with the fragrance of flowers. . . . Who cannot see that it all speaks of the celestial mysteries?"[7] In spring, as the poet

---

[7] St. Zeno of Verona, *Tractatus* I, 33 (CCL 22, 84).

Venantius Fortunatus similarly remarked, a mysterious rebirth pervades nature; a spark of life is in all living creatures: the bird, which was silent and sluggish in the winter's chill, is summoned back to song, and the "the bud swells in readiness for new growth."[8]

How beautiful it would be if the church could experience a similar moment of rebirth at Easter; if only during the Easter vigil at the celebrant's questions, "Do you believe in God the Father? Do you believe in Jesus Christ? Do you believe in the Holy Spirit?" we could all answer in a moment of joyful rapture and with the light of faith, "Yes, I do!"

St. Augustine writes, "Through his Passion the Lord passed from death to life, opening the path for us, if we *believe* in his resurrection, so we may also pass from death to life."[9] Faith, as one can see, is the secret to experience Easter in fullness, and to pass from death to life. It is the means by which we make Christ's Easter our own. Let us say, together with the man in the gospel, "I do believe, help my unbelief!" (Mark 9:24).

---

[8] Venantius Fortunatus, *Carmina,* III, 9 (PL 88, 131).
[9] St. Augustine, *De Cat. Rud.,* 23, 41, 3 (PL 40, 340).

3

THE MORAL SENSE TEACHES HOW TO ACT

Easter in Life

1. From faith to virtue

"The *letter* teaches the facts; *allegory* what to believe; the *moral* sense teaches how to act; and the *anagogical* what to aim at." *(Littera gesta docet, quid credas allegoria. / Moralis quid agas; quo tendas anagogia.)* We have reached the third level of the reading of the Scriptures, i.e., the moral one, which draws from Easter practical teachings for daily life and mores.

Worth noticing is the order with which these different senses of the Bible follow one another; morals do not come before mystery, and deeds do not precede faith, but the opposite. St. Gregory the Great's principle is thus kept unaltered: "One does not go from virtue to faith; one goes from faith to virtue."[1]

Unfortunately, at a certain point this order was altered. To some fathers of the church it seemed more correct, from a pedagogic point of view, to deal with morals first and then with the more elevated, mystical realm. Hence, St. Ambrose suggested a new order: first history, second morals, and finally mystery.[2] This tendency was reinforced by the fact that active life was generally associated with morals, and contemplative life with mystery. Besides, it is well known that in the Middle Ages contemplative life, symbolized by Mary, was considered superior to active life, symbolized by Martha. Later, when it became common practice to distinguish in spiritual life the three famous stages (purgative, illuminative, and unitive or mystical), morals, which preside over the purgative,

[1] St. Gregory the Great, *Homily on Ezechiel,* II, 7 (PL 76, 1018).
[2] St. Ambrose, *Commentary on the Gospel according to St. Luke,* III, 35 (PL 15, 1603): *historiam, mores, mysterium.*

could not but precede, in commenting on the Scriptures, the focus on mystery.

Therefore, in practice if not in theory, deeds came before faith, and morals before the *kerygma*.[3] This would also help create that situation which provided Luther with a cue for his radical protest. According to him, Christ is not a model to imitate in one's own life but a gift to be received through faith, period. It was the birth of the dispute on faith and deeds, which was destined to go on for a long time and create so many conflicting points of view.

Today, an agreement has been reached (at least on this point) with the document co-signed by the Catholic and the Lutheran World Federation. No more faith or deeds, but both faith and deeds, though each in the right order. In the end, it was what St. Gregory the Great had enunciated in his maxim, "One does not go from virtue to faith; one goes from faith to virtue."

2. Clear out the old yeast

The moral reading pertinent to Easter has a long history. Paul the Apostle wrote to the Corinthians, "Clear out the old yeast so that you may become a fresh batch of dough, inasmuch as you are unleavened. For our paschal lamb, Christ, has been sacrificed. Therefore, let us celebrate the feast, not with the old yeast, the yeast of malice and wickedness, but with the unleavened bread of sincerity and truth" (1 Cor 5:7-8).

There is good evidence that Paul the Apostle wrote these words as Easter approached, presumably in the year 57. The exhortation "let us celebrate the feast" as a matter of fact refers to Easter celebration, which now is no longer experienced only in memory of the sacrifice of the lamb and the flight from Egypt, but also and above all in memory of Christ's sacrifice. It is the most ancient evidence of the existence of a Christian Passover, "our Easter."

Paul the Apostle's exhortation is therefore the first "lenten" sermon of Christianity. He takes his cue from the Jewish tradition of cleaning the household and getting rid of every crumb of leavened

---

[3] Henri de Lubac, *Exégèse médiévale. Les quatre sens de l'Ecriture,* I,2 (Paris: Aubier, 1959) 413; Engl. transl. *Medieval Exegesis: The Four Senses of Scripture,* I/2, trans. Mark Sebanc (Grand Rapids: William B. Eerdmans Publishing Company, 1998).

bread, to illustrate the moral implications of Christian Easter. Similarly, Christians must clean the interior household of their hearts to destroy all that belongs to the old regime of sin and corruption.

The subsequent development of the doctrine and praxis of the church has established where and how Easter purification must take place, and how to get rid of "the old yeast": by means of the sacrament of reconciliation. Applying to Easter the four-part scheme we have been following in these meditations, a medieval author wrote, "Easter can have an historical, allegorical, moral, and anagogical meaning. *Historically,* Easter took place when the Angel of death struck down all the first-born in Egypt; *allegorically,* when the church, in baptism, passes from disbelief to faith; *morally,* when the soul, through confession and contrition, passes from sin to virtue; *anagogically,* when we pass from the miseries of this life to heavenly joy."[4]

The close link between Easter and confession was canonically sanctioned in 1215 by the Lateran Council, which established confession and communion at least at Easter.[5] In *Novo Millennio Ineunte* the Pope exhorts us to "propose the practice of the sacrament of reconciliation in a persuasive and effective way."[6] I am not sure I will be able to be so "persuasive and effective"; I wish, however, to accept the invitation to say a few words which may rekindle in us the desire of a good Easter confession.

First of all, let us remember that in our daily struggle against sin the sacrament of reconciliation is not the only means at our disposal. The fathers and doctors of the church have acknowledged the Eucharist as thoroughly effective in delivering us from sin.[7] The blood of Christ we receive on that occasion purifies "our consciences from dead works," as the letter to the Hebrews assures us (Heb 9:14). St. Ambrose wrote, "For as often as you drink, you receive the remission of sins and you are inebriated in Spirit." Moreover, he added, "This bread is the remission of sins."[8] Before

---

[4] Sicard of Cremona, *Mitrale,* VI, 15 (PL 213, 543).

[5] See *Conciliorum Oecumenicorum Decreta* (Bologna, 1973) 245, trans. Rev. H. J. Schroeder, O.P., *Disciplinary Decrees of the General Councils, Text, Translation, and Commentary* (St. Louis: B. Herder, 1937).

[6] Apostolic Letter *Novo millennio ineunte,* 6 January 2001, 37.

[7] See St. Thomas Aquinas, *S. Th. III* q. LXXIX, a a. 3-6.

[8] St. Ambrose, *De sacr.* V, 3, 17 (CSEL 73) 65; *De ben. Patr.* 9, 39 (CSEL 32, 2) 147.

distributing the Eucharistic bread the celebrant pronounces the liturgical formula, "Behold the Lamb of God who takes away the sins of the world." According to the fathers, the petition of the Our Father, "forgive us our trespasses," is also another way to be forgiven of our sins.

However, we know that the traditional and fundamental way to be forgiven of our deadly sins committed after baptism is the sacrament of reconciliation, which is also an excellent instrument to deliver us from our venial sins as well as common faults. We all know very well the historical and theological principles related to this sacrament and largely illustrated in the post-synodal exhortation *Reconciliation and Penance* of 1984. Nevertheless, I would like to add just a few other remarks of an existential and spiritual kind.

Confession is the moment in which the dignity of the individual believer is most clearly affirmed. In every other moment of the life of the church the believer is one among many: one of those who listen to the Word, one of those who receive the Eucharist. At confession, there is one and only one person; on that occasion the church is there entirely for him/her.

This way of freeing oneself from sin by confessing it to God's minister corresponds to the natural need of the human psyche to be released of that which oppresses the conscience by manifesting it, bringing it out into light, and giving it verbal expression. Psalm 32 is about the joy brought about by such an experience:

Happy the sinner whose fault is removed,
Whose sin is forgiven.
Happy those to whom the LORD imputes no guilt,
In whose spirit is no deceit.

As long as I kept silent, my bones wasted away;
I groaned all the day.
For day and night your hand was heavy upon me;
My strength withered as in dry summer heat.

Then I declared my sin to you;
My guilt I did not hide.
I said, "I confess my faults to the LORD,"
And you took away the guilt of my sin (Ps 32:1-5).

3. A spiritual renewal of the sacrament

In order to be truly effective in the battle against sin, the sacrament of penance, as everything else in the church, must undertake a spiritual renewal in the way it is dispensed as well as received. The link between the Spirit and the forgiveness of sins is in the very same words as the institution of this sacrament, "Receive the holy Spirit. Whose sins you forgive are forgiven them, and whose sins you retain are retained" (John 20:22).

An ancient liturgical prayer affirms, "We pray you, Lord: may the Holy Spirit heal our souls with the divine sacraments, for He himself is the forgiveness of all sins."[9] This bold statement was inspired by St. Ambrose's words. "In the forgiveness of sins," writes the saint, "men exercise a ministry but not through any power of their own; for it is through the Holy Spirit (alone) that sins are forgiven."[10]

One of the symbols of the Holy Spirit is fire, "He will baptize you with the holy Spirit and fire" (Matt 3:11); "Then there appeared to them tongues as of fire . . . and they were all filled with the holy Spirit" (Acts 2:3-4). Fire purifies. Water also symbolizes purification, but with a difference: water purifies only superficially, whereas fire purifies in depth "to the marrow," and frees from dross. Gold is purified not by washing it in water, but by passing it through a furnace. The Holy Spirit does the same in the sacrament of reconciliation: God's image is purified from the dirt of sin, regaining thus its original splendor. Talking about the live coal which purifies Isaiah's mouth, St. Ambrose wrote, "That fire was a type of the Holy Spirit who was to come down after the Lord's ascension, and forgive the sins of all, and who like fire inflames the soul and mind of the faithful."[11]

A spiritual renewal of the sacrament of penance means to experience confession not as a rite, a practice, or a canonical obligation to be observed, but rather as a personal encounter with the Risen One, and, like Thomas, to touch his wounds, feel deep within oneself the healing power of his blood, and taste "the joy of salvation." Confession enables us to experience within ourselves

---

[9] Roman Missal, Tuesday after Pentecost.

[10] St. Ambrose, *On the Holy Spirit*, III, 137.

[11] St. Ambrose, *On Duties*, III, 18, 103 (PL 16, 174).

what the church sings at the Easter vigil in the *Exsultet,* "O happy fault which gained for us so great a Redeemer!" Jesus knows how to make of all human faults, once they have been acknowledged, "happy faults," faults no longer remembered but for the experience of divine mercy and tenderness which they occasioned!

A greater miracle than saying to a paralytic "Rise . . . and walk" takes place in every absolution (see Mark 2:9). Only divine power can create from nothing that which is not, and reduce to nothing that which is, and this is precisely what takes place in the forgiveness of sins. In it is achieved in fact that which in principle took place on the Cross: the "sinful body is done with" (Rom 6:6).

The sacrament of reconciliation provides us with an excellent and incomparable means to renew each time the experience of being gratuitously justified by faith. It re-enacts over and again the "wonderful exchange" between our sins offered to Christ and the justice he gives us. After every good confession we are like the publican who, for having only said, "Lord, have mercy on me a sinner!" returns home "justified," forgiven, and made a new creature.

Having received absolution we must be careful to not repeat the mistake of the nine lepers who do not even turn back to express their gratitude (see Luke 17:17). Let us consider the sinful woman whose sins are forgiven because she shows such great love for Jesus: how devotedly and tenderly she kneels weeping, while her tears fall on Jesus' feet, and she wipes them away with her hair (see Luke 7:37). After every confession we also can run to the house where Jesus is invited to a meal—at the eucharistic table or in front of the Blessed Sacrament— and from the bottom of our hearts pour out all our overwhelming gratitude.

Moreover, a spiritual renewal of the sacrament means to revise every now and then the *object* of our confessions as well. The danger here is to be entrenched in old schemes of examining our consciences learned when we were young, and to continue them in our adult life, despite the fact that situations have changed and our real sins are no longer the same as they were then.

At times, when there are no serious sins to confess, I think that we should get rid of all our schemes and, preparing ourselves for confession, have a little conversation with Jesus, such as this, "Jesus, in confidence just between you and me: what is it that in this period has displeased you most in me, what has saddened and offended you?" Usually, the answer to this question is not very slow in coming. Once we know it, we must get to the point and not bury it, during confession, under a long list of habitual faults.

4. Penitents and confessors

Many of us here gathered are not only penitents, but also confessors; we not only receive the sacrament of reconciliation, we also administer it. The renewal of the sacrament is not only related to the way of receiving it, but also to the way of administering it. At this point, allow me in all humility to share some thoughts on the subject.

The Latin Church has tried to explain this sacrament with the juridical idea of a trial from which one emerges either absolved or not absolved. In such a trial, the minister holds the office of judge. This view, if accentuated unilaterally, can have negative consequences: it becomes difficult to recognize Jesus in the confessor. In the parable of the prodigal son, the father does not behave like a judge, but exactly like a father; even before the son has finished making his confession, he embraces him and orders a feast. The Gospel is the true "Manual for Confessors"; canon law is there to serve it, not to replace it.

Jesus does not begin by asking in an imperious tone the adulteress, Zaccheus, and all the sinners he meets "the number and kind" of their sins: "How many times? With whom? Where?" His main concern is for the person to experience God's compassion and tenderness—even God's joy in welcoming the sinner. He knows that after this experience the sinners themselves will feel the need of an ever more complete confession of their faults. Throughout the whole Bible we see in action the pedagogy of God which does not demand from men and women everything at once in matters of morality, but only that which at the moment they are able to understand. Paul the Apostle speaks of a "forbearance of God" (see Rom 3:26). The essential point here is the presence of true contrition and the willingness to change and make amendment.

John Paul II has stressed this aspect, and not only in the encyclical *Dives in misericordia*. In 1983, while the Episcopal synod on *Penance and Reconciliation in the Mission of the Church* was still in process, he decided to proclaim the canonization, in the presence of the entire synod, of Blessed Leopold Mandic, a humble Capuchin friar who spent his life hearing confessions. Well known is the affability, the love and the encouragement with which St. Leopold welcomed and dismissed every penitent. To those who used to criticize him for being "too good," hinting that God would ask him to explain his excessive generosity with penitents, he used to reply, "We were not the ones who died for souls, but He poured out His divine blood. Therefore, we must treat souls as He has taught us with his example. If the Lord were to reproach me for too much generosity, I could say to him, 'Blessed Lord, You gave me this bad example.'"[12]

The results attest to the goodness of this way of administering the sacrament. At a distance of half a century, one still finds in Italy people who give credit to him for their return to the church. It is true that together with St. Leopold, most tender in his ministry as confessor, there is St. Pio of Pietrelcina, of the same order, notable at times for his grumpy manners in receiving and dismissing penitents. But to imitate him in this, one would have to be sure of having the same gift that he had of binding souls in this way closer to himself and making them return to his confessional immediately afterward, with a changed disposition of heart.

Pietro Palazzini, in those days the cardinal prefect of the Congregation of Saints, in his presentation of a book on St. Leopold, wrote, "If there are persons who have the primary obligation of saving confession from the crisis which seems to threaten it, these are, above all, priests . . . if the falling away of faithful from this most human and comforting sacrament occurred as a result of other causes, it would be painful . . . ; but it would never be as painful as when the ministers themselves were the ones to blame."[13] It is not unusual to meet people who have been away from confession for years, and at times for their whole lives, after a traumatic meeting which took place the last time they approached the sacrament.

The administration of penance for a confessor can become an occasion of conversion and grace, as the proclamation of the Word of God is for the preacher. In the penitent's sins he recognizes

---

[12] Lorenzo da Fara, *Leopoldo Mandic. L'umanita', la santita'* (Padova: 1987) 103f.

[13] Various authors, *In nome della misericordia. Leopoldo Mandic e la confessione oggi* (Padova: Portavoce di S. Leopoldo, 1990) 8.

without difficulty, perhaps in different forms, his own sins, and while he hears a confession he cannot but say within himself, "Lord, so am I, so did I, have mercy on me as well." How many sins, never included in one's own examination of conscience, are revealed while listening to the sins of others! To some penitents more afflicted, St. Leopold would say to encourage them, "Here we are, two sinners: God have mercy on us!"[14]

I would like to end this meditation with a poem by Paul Claudel in which he describes confession with the same images used in the liturgy celebrating Christ's resurrection. It rekindles our joy in looking forward to Easter, spiritually renewed by a good confession:

> My God, I am raised and I am again with You!
> I was asleep and lying like a dead person in the night.
> God said, "Let there be light!" and I woke up
> As a cry is uttered!
> I am raised and I have awakened,
> I am standing up and I start with the day that begins!
> My father, who created me before the dawn,
> I place myself in Your presence,
> My heart is free and my mouth is clear,
> My body and spirit are empty.
> I am absolved of all my sins,
> Which I have confessed one by one.
> The wedding ring is on my finger and my face is clean.
> I am like an innocent being in the grace
> That you have granted me.[15]

---

[14] da Fara, *Leopoldo Mandic,* 106.

[15] Paul Claudel, *Corona benignitatis anni Dei, Oeuvres poetiques* (Paris: Gallimard, 1967) 377:

"Mon Dieu, je suis ressuscité et je suis encore avec Toi!
Je dormais et j'étais couché ainsi qu'un mort dans la nuit.
Dieu dit: Que la lumière soit! et je me suis réveillé comme on pousse un cri!
J'ai surgi et je me suis réveillé, je suis debout et je commence avec le jour qui commence!
Mon père qui m'avez engendré avant l'Aurore, je me place dans Votre Présence.
Mon cœur est libre et ma bouche est nette, mon corps et mon esprit sont à jeun.
Je suis absous de tous mes péchés que j'ai confessés un par un.
L'anneau nuptial est à mon doigt et ma face est nettoyée.
Je suis comme un être innocent dans la grâce
que Vous m'avez octroyée."

4

PASSING OVER
TO WHAT NEVER PASSES

Eternal Easter

1. Easter as ascent

The patristic and biblical tradition has interpreted the paschal notion of "passage" in several ways: "passing over" *(hyperbasis)*, "crossing over" *(diabasis)*, "ascent" *(anabasis)*, "way out" *(exodus)*, and "progress" *(progressio)*. Easter means "passing over" when it indicates God, or God's angel, "passing over" and sparing the Israelites' houses; it is a "crossing over" when it refers to the Israelites' fleeing from Egypt toward the promised land, and from slavery to freedom; an "ascent" when men and women rise from worldly matters to what is above; a "way out" or exodus when men and women escape the prison of sin; a "progress" when they advance in holiness and virtue.

In this last meditation I would like to reflect on the passage to what is above. Origen suggests that Easter is always "ascending"; Jesus celebrated it "in the upper room," therefore Christians must also "ascend" if they want to celebrate Easter with him. "No one who wants to celebrate Easter with Jesus would stay on the lower floor."[1]

Let us recall once again the famous Latin distich, *"History* teaches the facts; *allegory* what to believe; the *moral* sense teaches how to act, and the *anagogical* what to aim at." The literal meaning of the word *anagogy* is lifting up, rising, ascent. In its Christian connotation it refers to the wide field of the "not yet," separate from what has been "already" accomplished by Christ's life and the church; in other words, it points to the eschatological tension of Christian life.

---

[1] Origen, *Homily on Jeremiah,* 19, 13 (GCS 2, 239f.).

The *anagogical* has taken two distinct directions: one is the *speculative*, which consists in a theological reflection on the ultimate events (the theological treatise on "the last things"), the other is the *practical*, a concrete aiming at the last things, being constantly "oriented toward the eternal gifts." St. Augustine well illustrated the difference between the two when he said that if you want to cross a stretch of sea, you don't stay on the shore and look at the horizon to guess what is on the other side; rather, you get in a boat and go in that direction.[2]

It is well known to what extent the eschatological tension was present in Christ's discourses and in the first Christian community. The Eucharist itself is celebrated "until he comes" (1 Cor 11:26). A look at history will help us determine when and how this confident expectation became part of the Easter celebration and shaped its spirit and content.

2. Easter and expectation

St. Jerome refers to an apostolic tradition according to which Christ would return in the middle of Easter night; he actually says that it is wrong to dismiss churchgoers before midnight of the Easter vigil. There was the chance that before the midnight hour Christ could return in glory, just as he said he would (see Matt 25:6; Mark 13:35).[3] Lactantius is the first to attest to this tradition by stating, "This is the night that we shall celebrate watching for the advent of our King and God. It has a double meaning: on that night he regained life after his passion, and on that night he will regain his kingship of the earth."[4]

There existed in ancient Christianity, therefore, a tradition that associated Easter with *parousia* in chronological terms. Yet, already by the end of the second century the attitude toward this situation had changed. From the "second coming," or Christ's return, attention shifted to his first coming, namely his incarnation. In other words, attention shifted from the future to the past. This change was caused by the heresy of Docetism, as well as by Gnos-

---

[2] See St. Augustine, *The Trinity,* IV, 15, 20; *The Confessions,* VII, 21.

[3] See St. Jerome, *In Matthaeum,* IV, 25, 6.

[4] Lactantius, *Divinae instit.* VII, 19, 3.

ticism's attempt to deprive the historical events of Christ's earthly life of their meaning, reducing them to mere appearance.

In this context Christian authors of the second century considered particularly appropriate John's eschatology of the "already accomplished," which locates the decisive point in history not ahead, in the accomplishment of the end, but in the past, in the fundamental event of Christ's incarnation and salvific death, which have already inaugurated the last days. Both memory and expectation would continue to be at the heart of Christian Easter, but the emphasis is at this point definitely given to the former. Easter, like the Eucharist, is fundamentally "memorial" of Christ's death and resurrection. The waiting for Christ's imminent return takes now the shape of a constant longing for "what is above." Hence, the anagogical emerges: "After allegory, which edifies faith, and the moral sense, which edifies charity, comes the anagogical, which edifies hope."[5]

In this sense it can be said that the Christian paschal vigil is a "liturgy" of hope. Its focus—ever since every millenarian anxiety has been discharged—is essentially transcendental. According to Origen, Easter is celebrated when "the mysteries of the future century are revealed, and the soul's hope, free from worldly concerns, is projected above and anchored to what eye never saw, ear never heard, and is still unknown to the human heart."[6]

In this new context hope becomes the core of the paschal vigil. The act itself of being vigilant is emblematic of waiting for the Lord's coming, which must characterize the entire life of Christians. St. Augustine writes:

> In our vigil we do not wait for the Lord as though he still has to rise from the dead, but rather we solemnly renew each year the memory of his resurrection. However, in this celebration we recall the past so that by means of our vigil we may give expression to what we do in life through faith. All this time in fact, in which the current age passes like a night, the church waits with

[5] Henri de Lubac, *Exégèse médiévale. Les quatre sens de l'Ecriture*, I,2 (Paris: Aubier, 1959) 623; Engl. transl. *Medieval Exegesis: The Four Senses of Scripture* I/2, trans. Mark Sebanc (Grand Rapids: William B. Eerdmans Publishing Company, 1998).

[6] Origen, *Homily on Numbers*, 23, 6 (GCS 7, 218).

the eyes of faith focused on the Scriptures as on torches shining
in the dark, until the day of the coming of the Lord.[7]

As can be seen, Augustine never separates the *expectation* of what
will be from the *memory* of what was. According to him, paschal joy itself flows from these two combined movements of the
soul—and it flows abundantly:

> *Brothers, what a joy! Joy in being gathered here together; joy
> in singing psalms and hymns; joy in the memory of Christ's
> Passion and Resurrection; joy in the hope of the future life. If
> so much joy gives us hope, what then will be its possession? In
> these days, when we hear resonating the Alleluia, our spirit is
> like transfigured. Don't we feel like savoring something of that
> celestial city?*[8]

Every Easter brings the church closer to our Lord's *parousia*,
without separating it from the crib of redemption from which it
was born. St. Zeno of Verona writes, "The day of Easter is per-
petually on the run toward old age, and yet it never leaves the crib
in which it was born."

"It is both heir and father of centuries"; "It is the day that antici-
pates what will be," the day which, the older it gets, the younger it
seems for the approach of the finish line.[9]

Following in the footsteps of St. Augustine, paschal theology
reached an unsurpassed balance between *memory, presence,* and
expectation in the celebration of the Easter vigil. "The Easter we
celebrate," writes an author influenced by Augustine, "makes *past
present* and is oriented toward the *future* of resurrection."[10] The
liturgical celebration of Easter has kept alive in the heart of the
church the eschatological tension, even afterwards, when it expressed more the vivid hope for eternal Easter than the anxious
expectation of the *parousia*.

---

[7] St. Augustine, *Sermo Wilmart,* 4, 3 (PLS II, 718).

[8] St. Augustine, *Sermo Morin-Guelferbytanus,* 8, 2 (PLS II, 577).

[9] St. Zeno of Verona, *De Pascha, Tract.* I, 33, 58; 11, 13 (CC 22, 84, 133, 187);
De Pascha Tract. I, 16, 44 (CC 22, 63, 117) *("longaeva semper aetate novellus").*

[10] Pseudo Augustine, *Sermo Caillau-Saint-Yves,* I, App. 3 (PLS II, 1020).

3. Seeking what is above

After this historical outline we may ask a practical question: how can the vertical dimension of Easter, the one oriented toward the heavenly Jerusalem, be experienced? The idea of Easter implies the notion of "passage," *transitus;* this word conjures up something ephemeral, "transitory," therefore negative. St. Augustine perceived this problem and solved it in an insightful way. In his explanation to celebrate Easter does not merely mean to pass, but to "pass to what never passes," meaning, "to pass over this world, in order not to pass away with it."[11]

To fully understand such a definition in all its potential implications the transitory nature of life must be once for all clearly acknowledged. An ancient philosopher, Heraclitus, put into words this fundamental experience with a famous maxim: *panta rei,* i.e., everything flows. As it is on the TV screen, so it is in life: programs flow rapidly, replacing one another. The screen stays the same, but the running images change. The same happens to us: the world remains, but we pass away, one generation after the next. In a few years, what will remain of all the names, the faces, the news in the daily papers and the TV programs—what of me, you, all of us? Absolutely nothing. Men and women are just "shapes drawn by the waves on the seashore obliterated by the next incoming tide."

In the attempt to endure and not completely die some of us cling to youth and love, others to their children or fame. The poet Horace declared, "I won't completely die. I built (with my poems) a monument more stable than bronze." True, but what good does it do him? It is good for us, but not for him. As the Bible puts it, "All mortals are but a breath. Mere phantoms we go our way; mere vapor, our restless pursuits; we heap up stores without knowing for whom" (Ps 39:6-7), and I assume that, at least on this point, we all agree with the psalmist.

At the very moment of birth an incessant countdown starts for all of us. Once in our friaries we used to have enormous pendulum-clocks with the following chiseled, admonishing words: *Vulnerant omnes, ultima necat.* Each one (i.e., the hours) hurts, the last kills.

---

[11] St. Augustine, *In Ioh* 55, 1 (CCL 36, 463f.).

Confronted with the experience that everything passes away, the approaches that can be taken are various. One, very old and mentioned in the Bible itself, says, "Eat and drink, for tomorrow we die!" (Isa 22:13). Recalling the days preceding the deluge, Jesus said, "they were eating, drinking, marrying and giving in marriage . . . They did not know until the flood came and carried them all away" (Matt 24:38).

What does faith have to tell us about this fact that everything passes away? "Yet the world and its enticement are passing away. But whoever does the will of God remains forever" (1 John 2:17). There is, therefore, someone who does not pass away, i.e., God, and there is also for us a way not to pass completely away: by doing the will of God, i.e., believing and clinging to God. One of the recurring images in the Bible refers to God as the Rock: "The Rock . . . how just and upright he is!" (Deut 32:4). I realized what these words of God meant the day in which, for the first time, I saw the Matterhorn at close quarters.

In this life we are like people on a raft, carried by the waters of a river in flood toward the open sea from where there is no return. At a certain point the raft comes very close to the shore. The survivors say, "Now or never again!" and jump on the dry ground. What a relief it is when their feet touch the solid land! Those who land on the shores of faith are left with the same impression. This is what "to pass over to what never passes" means: to pass *over* the world—not away *with* it.

4. Why are you standing there looking at the sky?

Looking forward to accomplish this passage with our body on the last day, Christians must complete it every day within their *hearts*. But does this passing of the heart to what never passes dissuade Christians from their historical duties in this world? Well known are the accusations against believers in this respect. Hegel said, "Christians waste in heaven the treasures destined for their lives on earth!" Similarly, Karl Marx declared, "They project in heaven their unfulfilled desires on earth."

To answer back to these objections, we take our cue from the story of Christ's Ascension. It is interesting to hear from the "two men dressed in white garments" who appeared to the apostles the same objection which, in a less friendly tone, has been often used by non-believers addressing Christians: "Men of Galilee, why are you standing there looking at the sky?" (Acts 1:11).

First of all, let us make clear the meaning of the word "sky" in Christian language, and its relation with the present life on earth. Let us start with Plato's famous myth of the cave. Figure this scene, says the philosopher. Some men have been kept in the darkness of a deep cave, with their shoulders to the entrance. They are tied up in such a way they can only look ahead, at the wall, in the back of the cave. At their shoulders, behind a low wall, people are coming and going with various objects in their hands or on their heads. Between the entrance of the cave and the people carrying their objects there is a fire projecting their shadows on the wall in the back of the cavern, the only one the captives can see. In their whole life they have never seen anything else, therefore they believe that the shadows are the only reality, that there is nothing else. So much so that even if one of them finally manages to escape and go outside, when he later comes back to tell his comrades how things really are, they will put him to death in the belief that too much light has driven him insane. (Here Plato alludes to what the Athenians did to Socrates!)

According to Plato, this is the condition of the human family in the world. The world is a cave. What we regard as true and real are but shadows of reality which reside above in the sky, mere copies of celestial realities. A true knowledge of reality requires detaching ourselves from the corporeal, which keeps us clinging to matter and illusions, and "going outside the cave." Raphael has masterfully epitomized Plato's vision in the painting called *The School of Athens*. The two most influential philosophers of the ancient world, Plato and Aristotle, are here represented in two contrasting manners. Aristotle's hand is turned to the ground, as though he is saying that reality is on earth and that our knowledge should stem from what we see and touch. By contrast, Plato, with his finger pointed upward, reminds us that reality is above, in the sky.

There are sentences of the Scriptures that seem to be modeled on the Platonic vision of reality, as illustrated in the myth of the cave. The figure in Raphael's painting, with his finger pointing to the sky, could well be St. Paul the Apostle himself when he says, "If then you were raised with Christ, seek what is above, where

Christ is seated at the right hand of God. Think of what is above, not of what is on earth" (Col 3:1-2). Is Christian faith, then, just a modernized version of Platonism? Did the coming of Christ mean nothing at all? In reality, there is just one, substantial difference; the sky for Christians is not the one conceived by Plato. When we talk about the sky, neither do we think of a *place* above us, nor a superior world of ideas, or *hyperouranios;* what we intend is an *event* ahead of us. After asking the apostles, "Why are you standing there looking at the sky?" the two angels tell them the right direction they should turn to, i.e., toward the day when the Lord will come back: "This Jesus who has been taken up from you into heaven will return in the same way as you have seen him going into heaven" (Acts 1:11). St. Paul the Apostle states the same: "But our citizenship is in heaven, and from it we also wait a savior, the Lord Jesus Christ" (Phil 3:20).

The sky of Christian faith is, in conclusion, a *person:* the risen Christ with whom we will be united after our resurrection in "one body" and, though in a temporary and incomplete manner, already after our death. To go to "heaven" or to the "celestial home" means "be with Christ" (Phil 1:23). Jesus said, "I am going to prepare a place for you . . . so that where I am you also may be" (John 14:2-3).

This really changes everything. In Plato's eyes, the world had lost all its value; it was for him a cave, namely a prison. To escape, to run away from the world becomes, in this case, the password. There was no salvation *of* the flesh and *of* the world, but only *from* the flesh and *from* the world. The same does not apply for Christians. The body is not merely a "medium" or "vessel" to leave behind. Its destiny is to partake, with the soul, in glory. "This life is so sweet,"[12] we all wish to be happy in this body of ours, not *without* it; faith assures us that this is how it will be.

In addition: if creation, as God's own work, is also awaiting glorious freedom (see Rom 8:19), then not only are we called to be concerned about its fate but also about its safekeeping and growth. There is no need to escape from this world to be with the Lord, for the Lord is already in this world: "And behold, I am with you always, until the end of the age" (Matt 28:20).

---

[12] St. Augustine, *Sermones* 335B (Misc. Agostiniana, 1) 561.

Far from ignoring our responsibility to improve the conditions of life in this world our faith in Christ's return and in eternal life becomes a remarkable incentive leaving no room for complacent indolence. As St. Paul the Apostle used to say, we are given time to "do good to all" (Gal 6:10). "Waste in heaven the treasures destined for this life on earth," indeed! Christians do have their eyes fixed on watching the sky; but they also have solid ground beneath their feet.

Someone may ask, "But, what shall we do 'in heaven' with Christ for eternity, since it is there that we are destined to go? Aren't we going to be bored?" To such questions I would like to reply: is it boring to be happy and enjoy good health? Ask lovers if it is boring to be together. When we experience a moment of pure and extremely intense joy, don't we want it to last forever? Here below, such moments never last long for there is nothing that can permanently satisfy us. With God it is different. Our minds will contemplate Truth and Beauty everlastingly, while our hearts will never grow tired of delighting in Goodness.

I would like to conclude with a nice story. Once upon a time in a medieval monastery there were two monks who were great friends. One's name was Rufus, the other's Rufinus. Whenever they had a spare moment they could not but try to imagine and describe how life would be in the heavenly Jerusalem. Rufus, who was a master builder, imagined it as a city with golden gates studded with precious gems; Rufinus, who was an organist, imagined it resonating with celestial melodies. In the end, they made a bet: whoever died first would have to come back the following night and tell the other if it were exactly as they imagined. One single word would suffice: if it were as they thought then the word would be *"taliter,"* i.e., *"you're right";* otherwise (though they considered it impossible) *"aliter,"* i.e., *"you're wrong."*

One evening, while he was playing the organ, Rufinus' heart stopped beating. His friend waited the whole night in trepidation, but nothing happened; he waited then for many weeks and months, fasting and staying awake at night, but nothing ever happened. Finally, on the anniversary of his death, Rufinus came at night to his friend's cell in a radiant halo. As he kept silent, it was Rufus who spoke first, asking the question whose answer he was sure of, *"taliter?"* But his friend shook his head, "no." In a frenzy, Rufus then shouted, *"aliter?"* Again, his friend shook his head. Then, at last, in a whisper Rufinus uttered two words, *"Totaliter aliter,"* i.e., *"it's completely different!"* At once, not only did Rufus realize that heaven is infinitely greater than what they had imagined, but also impossible to describe, and shortly afterwards he died as well from too intense a longing to reach his friend.[13] Although the story is a tale, its content is really true.

One day, when we ascend to the real "upper room" where the eternal Easter is celebrated, I am sure that those two words: *Totaliter aliter!* (It's completely different!) will come spontaneously out of our mouths as well.

---

[13] See H. Franck, *Taliter?* in *Moderne Erzähler* (Paderborn, 1957) 37.

5

VICTOR QUIA VICTIMA

Victor because Victim

There is in physics a phenomenon called electric arc or voltaic arc. If two electrodes, one positive, the other negative, are set not too far apart, under particular environmental conditions they will release one of the brightest lights ever seen in nature.

Something similar occurs at every liturgy of the Word, but especially during the liturgy of Good Friday. The way is very simple; it consists in matching a passage from the Old with one from the New Testament, the prophecy with its fulfillment, which, in our case, is represented by the fourth Servant Song in Deutero-Isaiah and the narration of Christ's Passion. The whole is set at the right "temperature," represented by the faith and devout recollection of the church.

Let us, therefore, meditate on the Servant Song heard in the first reading in the light of the passion narrative proclaimed in the Gospel. The opening of the passage is a prologue set in heaven with God speaking; what follows is the people's monologue, as in the chorus of a Greek tragedy, reflecting on the events from which they draw their own conclusions; the passage ends with God's words, this time announcing the final verdict.

1. My servant shall prosper

The event is such that it cannot be rightly understood without starting from its epilogue; this is why God foretells its conclusion at the beginning: "See, my servant shall prosper, he shall be raised high and greatly exalted" (Isa 52:13). There are allusions to something which has never happened before, many startled nations, kings standing speechless: the horizon is widened toward an absoluteness and universality which no historical narration, not even that of the Gospels, could possibly reach, determined, as it is, by time and space. It is the intrinsic power of the prophecy that makes it precious and indispensable for us, even after we know the fulfillment of its truth.

At this point, the people begin to speak. First of all, almost to justify their blindness, they describe the Servant's unlikely appearance. He had no form or charm: how could we, they ask, discern "Yahweh's arm" in what was happening under our eyes?:

> He was spurned and avoided by men,
> A man of suffering, accustomed to infirmity,
> One of those from whom men hide their faces,
> Spurned, and we held him in no esteem (Isa 53:3).

But soon afterward comes the change of mind, the "revelation," the act of faith in its "nascent status":

> Yet it was our infirmities that he bore,
> Our sufferings that he endured,
> While we thought of him as stricken,
> As one smitten by God and afflicted.
> But he was pierced for our offenses,
> Crushed for our sins,
> Upon him was the chastisement that makes us whole,
> By his stripes we were healed (Isa 53:4-5).

To understand what happens at this point to the people, let us recall what happened when the prophecy became reality in Christ. For a while after Christ's death the only conviction about him was that he died, and died on the cross; that "God's curse [rested] on him" because it was written in the Law, "Cursed be everyone who hangs on a tree" (see Deut 21:23; Gal 3:13). As soon as the Holy Spirit came and "showed the world its sin" the paschal faith of the church began to blossom. Paul would proclaim, "Jesus our Lord . . . who was handed over for our transgressions and was raised for our justification" (Rom 4:25), and Peter testify, "He himself bore our sins in his body upon the cross" (1 Pet 2:24).

No one can stand on the Servant's side; he is completely set apart from the rest:

> We had all gone astray like sheep,
> Each following his own way,

> But the LORD laid upon him
> The guilt of us all (Isa 53:6).

The same prophet who writes puts himself among the "us." It would be wrong to think that he is talking about himself or another past figure without reducing the whole song to a set of pious exaggerations. Moreover, how can one believe the Servant to be a collectivity or a people if it is precisely for the sins of "his" people that he is struck down by death? As regards this Paul the Apostle will remove every doubt, "Jews and Greeks alike . . . are all under the domination of sin . . . all have sinned and are deprived of the glory of God" (Rom 3:9, 23).

The Bible provides us with a criterion to distinguish true from false prophecy: its fulfillment. A true prophecy is one which will be fulfilled, a false one will not (see Deut 18:21; Jer 28:9). This is a criterion that may take a long time to prove itself, but its outcome is certain. But where, when, or in whom was fulfilled that which is said of the Suffering Servant? Where are the many startled nations and the kings standing speechless? Who else but Christ has been for twenty centuries proclaimed without hesitation by billions of human beings, "He is my salvation! I have been healed by his wounds!"?

It is possible that some of the traits of the Servant are modeled on past figures such as Moses, Jeremiah, the prophet who wrote the Song, or the entire people of Israel; nevertheless, a complete identification can be guaranteed only in the life of Jesus of Nazareth. Before him, the Servant Song was like a musical score complete in every note, yet lacking any indication of the clef. Hence, we can understand the perplexity of the eunuch, the officer at the court of the candace or queen of Ethiopia, when he asks Philip the deacon, "I beg you, about whom is the prophet saying this? About himself, or about someone else?" After explaining the good news of Jesus, Philip baptized him (see Acts 8:26-40). The clef had finally been put in place.

2. But the LORD was pleased to crush him in infirmity

At this point, God begins again to speak:

> Because of his affliction
> He shall see the light in fullness of days;

> Through his suffering, my servant shall justify many,
> And their guilt he shall bear (Isa 53:11).

The most remarkable aspect of the entire Servant Song does not lie in the fact that the Servant remains meek as a sheep, without invoking God's justice and revenge, as, in similar circumstances, Job, Jeremiah, and several psalmists had done. The greatest novelty is that not even God is willing to vindicate the Servant and do him justice; better still, God's justice toward the Servant does not consist in punishing his persecutors, but rather in saving and justifying them! "My servant shall justify many."

This is what Paul the Apostle sees fulfilled in Christ, and triumphantly proclaims it in the letter to the Romans: "They are justified freely by his grace through the redemption in Christ Jesus, whom God set forth as an expiation" (Rom 3:24-25).

True, God's behavior toward the Servant in this event remains obscure: "But the LORD was pleased to crush him in infirmity" (Isa 53:10). We are horrified at the idea of a God who takes pleasure in tormenting the Son and, in general, any other creature. Yet, we may ask, "Did God really 'take pleasure' in it? What exactly was God's pleasure?" God did not take pleasure in the means but in the end! Not in the Servant's sufferings, but in his salvation of many. As St. Bernard put it, *"Non mors placuit sed voluntas sponte morientis";*[1] God did not take pleasure in the death of the Son, but in his willingness to die voluntarily for the salvation of the world.

What was indeed God's good pleasure and what God did with absolute joy is described in the following passage:

> Therefore I will give him his portion among the great,
> And he shall divide the spoils with the mighty,
> Because he surrendered himself to death
> And was counted among the wicked;
> And he shall take away the sins of many,
> And win pardon for their offenses (Isa 53:12).

---

[1] Bernard of Clairvaux, *De errore Abelardi*, 8, 21 (PL 182, 1070).

3. Beyond nonviolence

The Passion of Christ, prophetically described by Deutero-Isaiah and historically by the Gospels, offers a special message for our present time. The message is "Stop violence!" The Servant "had done no wrong" (Isa 53:9c), yet all the violence in the world converged on him: he was beaten up, pierced, abused, crushed, sentenced, removed from their midst, and finally dumped into a common grave ("A grave was assigned him among the wicked"; Isa 53:9). In all this he never uttered a cry; "like a lamb led to the slaughter, he was silent and opened not his mouth" (Isa 53:7). He offered himself as a sacrifice of reconciliation and "interceded" for his murderers, saying, "Father, forgive them, they know not what they do" (Luke 23:34). (Hence, we know that those who crucified Christ have been saved and are truly with him in heaven—at least those who really acted out of ignorance; for the Father, who always listened to him, could not have left unanswered his last prayer!)

Therefore, Christ has overcome violence; he has triumphed without answering violence with even greater violence. Instead, he suffered violence himself, thus revealing all its injustice and emptiness. He has inaugurated a new kind of victory which St. Augustine epitomized in three words, *"Victor quia victima"* (victor because victim).[2]

The question of violence haunts us, shocks us, now that it has created new and horrifying disguises of cruelty and obtuseness, and has also invaded the fields which should have been an antidote to it: sports, the arts, love. As Christians, we are horrified at the idea that one can do violence and kill in the name of God. Yet some argue, "But, isn't the Bible itself full of violent stories? Isn't God called 'Yahweh Sabaoth, Lord of armies'? Isn't the massacre of entire cities attributed to God? Isn't it God who imposes in the Mosaic Law many cases of the death penalty?"

Had this same argument been directed to Jesus during his lifetime he would certainly have replied with the same words he used in regard to divorce: "Because of the hardness of your hearts Moses allowed you to divorce your wives, but from the beginning it was not so" (Matt 19:8). Even in the case of violence, "it was not so

---

[2] St. Augustine, *Confessions*, X, 43.

from the beginning." The first chapter of Genesis presents us with a world where violence is not even conceivable, neither within the human family, nor between human beings and other animals. Murder is not permitted even to vindicate Abel's death (see Gen 4:15).

God's authentic view on the subject is expressed in the commandment "You shall not kill" (Exod 20:13) more than in the exceptions made to it in the Law, which are exceptions motivated by men's and women's mores and "hard-heartedness." By this time, violence is part of life, and the Bible, which tries to reflect life, attempts by means of its legislation (including the death penalty) at least to redirect and restrain violence so that it does not degenerate into an individual arbitrariness that would allow us to kill each other.[3]

Paul the Apostle mentions a time characterized by God's "forbearance" (Rom 3:25). God tolerates violence, as well as polygamy, divorce and other matters, but in the attempt to educate people in view of a time in which the original plan will be "recapitulated" and its glory restored, as it were, for a new creation. This time is fulfilled with Jesus who, on the mountain, proclaimed, "You have heard that it was said, 'An eye for an eye and a tooth for a tooth.' But I say this to you: offer no resistance to one who is evil. When someone strikes you on your right cheek, turn the other one to him as well. . . . You have heard that it was said, 'You shall love your neighbor and hate your enemy.' But I say to you, love your enemies and pray for those who persecute you" (Matt 5:38-39; 43-44).

Christ asserts his absolute and definitive "No" to violence, opposing to it not merely nonviolence, but more: forgiveness, meekness, and humility. "Take my yoke upon you and learn from me," he counsels, "for I am meek and humble of heart" (Matt 11:29). The true Sermon on the Mount, therefore, was not the one he gave that day on a mountain in Galilee but the one he gave silently on Mount Calvary in his hour of suffering.

If violence still persists, it can no longer, under any circumstances, be imputed to God and clothed in divine authority. That would entail the idea of a God identified with the crudest and most primitive stages of human development, which have now been overcome by humanity's religious and civic consciousness.

---

[3] See R. Girard, *Des choses cachées depuis la fondation du monde*, II, l'Ecriture judéo-chrétienne (Paris, 1981).

It is not even possible to justify violence in the name of progress. "Violence—as someone once put it—is history's midwife"
(Karl Marx and Friedrich Engels). In part, this is true. It is right to
say that, at times, new and more just social orders have stemmed
from revolutions and wars, but the opposite is also true: revolutions and wars have given rise to injustice and greater damage.

But this is precisely what reveals the state of confusion in which
the world at present exists: the fact that one has to resort to violence to correct evil, together with the assumption that what is
good can be achieved only by doing what is bad. Even those who
once were convinced of the fact that violence is "history's midwife" have changed their minds, and today parade in the streets in
the name of peace. Violence gives birth only to further violence.

Reflecting on the nonviolent events which in 1989 led to the fall
of the totalitarian regimes in Eastern Europe without bloodshed,
John Paul II, in the encyclical *Centesimus annus,* acknowledged
the significant role played in them by the men and women who,
without recourse to violence, bore witness to the truth. In his conclusion, he expressed a wish which, after fifteen years, resonates
ever more powerfully: "May the human family learn to struggle
for justice without violence."[4] I now would like to transform this
wish into a prayer:

"Lord Jesus Christ, we do not ask you to eliminate the violent
and those who boast of their ability to strike terror, but to change
their hearts and lead them back to you. Help us to say like you,
'Father, forgive them; they do not know what they are doing.' Dis-
solve this delirium of death and break the chain of violence and
hatred that keeps the world gasping for breath. You have created
the earth in peace and harmony; may it cease to be 'the flowerbed
which makes us so ferocious.'

"In the world there are innumerable human beings who like
you in your Passion 'have no appearance that would attract us;
spurned and avoided men and women of suffering, accustomed to
infirmity.' Teach us not to turn our faces at their sight, or shun
them, but to bear the burden of their sufferings and their solitude.

---

[4] John Paul II, Encyclical Letter On the Hundredth Anniversary of *Rerum no-
varum (Centesimus annus),* III, 23.

"Mary, 'by suffering as your Son was dying on the cross, you collaborated in a very singular way in the Savior's labor by your obedience, faith, hope, and burning charity'[5]: inspire men and women of our time with thoughts of peace and tenderness. And forgiveness. Amen."

[5] Dogmatic Constitution on the Church, *Lumen gentium*, 61.